Hawai'i

Shelley Gill

Illustrated by Scott Goto

ini Charlesbridge

To my wild woman hero, Sandy. I want to be just like you when I grow up—Shelley

For anyone who carries the ALOHA spirit in their hearts—Scott

Hawaiian Language

There are only 13 letters in the Hawaiian alphabet: A, E, H, I K, L, M, N, O, P, U, W, and ' ('okina). The Hawaiian language uses the following sounds:

Unstressed vowels
a as in aloud
e as in met
i as in the y in city
o as in mole
u as in June

Stressed vowels
a, ā as in jar
e as in met
ē as in the ay in clay
i, ī as in the ee in bee
o, ō as in mole
u, ū as in June

Consonants
h, k, l, m, n, and p sound as they do in English
w after i and e sounds like a v
w after u and o sounds like a w
w after a or at the start of a word can sound like either v or w

The 'okina (') is a glottal stop, like the sound between the ohs in "oh-oh." It is considered a consonant.

Here are some commonly used words in the Hawaiian language.

'a'ā sharp gravelly lava
'ahi yellowfin tuna
'āina land, earth
akamai smart, intelligent
ali'i Hawaiian royalty
aloha greeting used to say hello or goodbye. *Aloha* can also mean love.
'aumakua a personal god
'aumākua plural of *'aumakua*

hale house or home
hana work
Hana bay
haole foreigner
hapa portion; mix of races, such as *hapa haole*
hau'oli happy
he'e octopus. Also means to slide.
he'eia the sliding
heiau ancient Hawaiian religious temple on a raised base of lava rocks
holoholo to travel for fun
honu turtle
ho'okipa hospitality
huhū angry, agitated
hui group or organization
hula Hawaiian form of communication using dance

huli turn
humuhumu-nukunuku-āpua'a the state fish, Hawaiian triggerfish

imu underground pit oven used for cooking at a *lū'au*

kahiko traditional, ancient
kahuna Hawaiian priest
kāhuna plural of *kahuna*
kai ocean, saltwater
kālua to bake whole
kama'āina Native Hawaiian or long-time resident
kāne man
kapu forbidden, sacred
kaukau chant of lament
kōkua help
kino spirit of well-being
kui to string a *lei*
kupuna respected elder or grandparent

lani heavenly
laulau meat or fish and taro tops wrapped in ti leaves and steamed
lei garland of flowers, leaves, feathers, or shells
limu seaweed

lōlō crazy
lū'au Hawaiian feast

mahalo thank you
mahimahi dolphin fish
maika'i good
makahiki ancient Hawaiian celebration with sports and religious festivities
makai toward the ocean
malihini newcomer, visitor
mamo Hawaiian honeycreeper
manō shark
mauka toward the mountains
mauna mountain
mea kū'i'o fact
Menehune mythical race of small people who built fishponds, roads, and temples at night
mu'umu'u loose-fitting dress

nai'a porpoise
nēnē endangered Hawaiian goose
niu coconut

'ō'ō extinct honeyeater bird
'ono delicious

pāhoehoe smooth lava
pali cliff
palila Hawaiiian honeycreeper
pana celebrated place
paniolo cowboy
poi cooked and pounded taro root mixed with water
poke a Hawaiian dish made from octopus or fish
puka hole
pūlehu cook over hot coals
pūpū appetizer, snack
pupule crazy

uhu parrot fish
'ukulele small guitar

wahi place
wahine woman
wai freshwater
wikiwiki quick, fast

A little pidgin slang
auntie ma'am
brah buddy
da kine the real thing
'ōkole up butts up
'ono 'ono real good
uncle sir

Text copyright © 2006 by Shelley Gill
Illustrations copyright © 2006 by Scott Goto
All rights reserved, including the right of reproduction in whole or in part in any form. Charlesbridge and colophon are registered trademarks of Charlesbridge Publishing, Inc.

Published by Charlesbridge
85 Main Street
Watertown, MA 02472
(617) 926-0329
www.charlesbridge.com

Color separations by Chroma Graphics, Singapore
Printed and bound by Jade Productions

Library of Congress Cataloging-in-Publication Data
Gill, Shelley.
   Hawaii / Shelley Gill ; illustrated by Scott Goto.
     p. cm.
   ISBN-13: 978-0-88106-296-0; ISBN-10: 0-88106-296-0
(reinforced for library use)
   ISBN-13: 978-0-88106-297-7; ISBN-10: 0-88106-297-9 (softcover)
1. Hawaii—Juvenile literature. I. Goto, Scott, ill. II. Title.
DU623.25.G55 2006
996.9—dc22   2005006010

Printed in China
(hc) 10 9 8 7 6 5 4 3 2 1
(sc) 10 9 8 7 6 5 4 3 2 1

Aloha, brah!

Welcome to Hawai'i

My name is Patrick, but everybody calls me Uhu. That means parrot fish—the fish that eat coral and it comes out the other end as sand. Here on the islands when we have a picnic on the beach we say we're having *pūpū* on *uhu* doo-doo!

If I seem a bit excited, no worries. My dad and I have finished packing our kayaks. Tomorrow we start paddling around the Hawaiian Islands like my ancestors, the first people from the Marquesas Islands, did 1,500 years ago.

3

Ni'ihau   Kaua'i

Mea kū'i'o—Hawai'i became the 50th state on August 21, 1959. The native people of Hawai'i are called Hawaiians. Long-time residents are called "locals."

O'ahu

Moloka'i

Lāna'i   Maui

Kaho'olawe

Hawai'i

There are eight main islands in the Hawaiian chain: Hawai'i, Kaho'olawe, Maui, Lāna'i, Moloka'i, O'ahu, Kaua'i, and Ni'ihau. I live on Hawai'i—the Big Island. It is twice the size of all the other islands combined, and it has great bare lava beds, barren ash-covered slopes, tropical rain forests, waterfalls, and rolling grasslands.

In Hawaiian mythology, Pele is the goddess of Hawai'i's volcanoes. Pele was searching for a new home when she saw smoke and discovered an island, which she named Hawai'i. She climbed a mountain, then placed her magic stick into the ground at the top, creating Kīlauea Crater.

But why are there really volcanoes in the middle of the Pacific? Hot spots. Yeah, yeah, Hawai'i is hot, but we aren't talking weather here. There are hot spots in the earth's crust. When the lava explodes through them and flows out onto the sea floor, a seamount forms. Get it? A mountain under the sea. About a zillion years and many eruptions later, the mountain's layers pop out of the ocean and poof—an island! On the Big Island, Kīlauea is still active, and there has been an ongoing eruption of Mauna Loa for the past eight years.

You know you're in Hawai'i if . . .
you give directions using *mauka* and *makai*--
"mountainside" and "seaside."

Hawai'i

We're off! As we paddle through the shore break, I can see the snowcapped top of the tallest mountain in the world peeking through the clouds. If you thought we were looking at Mount Everest, think again. The tallest mountain in the world begins about 18,000 feet beneath the sea, then rises a whopping 32,000 feet to the summit. Only 13,796 feet stick out of the ocean to form the mountain known as Mauna Kea. The *palila* is a small yellow bird that lives only on the slopes of Mauna Kea.

At dawn we hike the short trail down to Pu'ukoholā Heiau. This temple was built in 1790–1791 by King Kamehameha I of Hawai'i, also known as Kamehameha the Great. It is where Kamehameha's last great rival—his cousin—was killed. After conquering all the islands, Kamehameha I united them and became the first Hawaiian monarch.

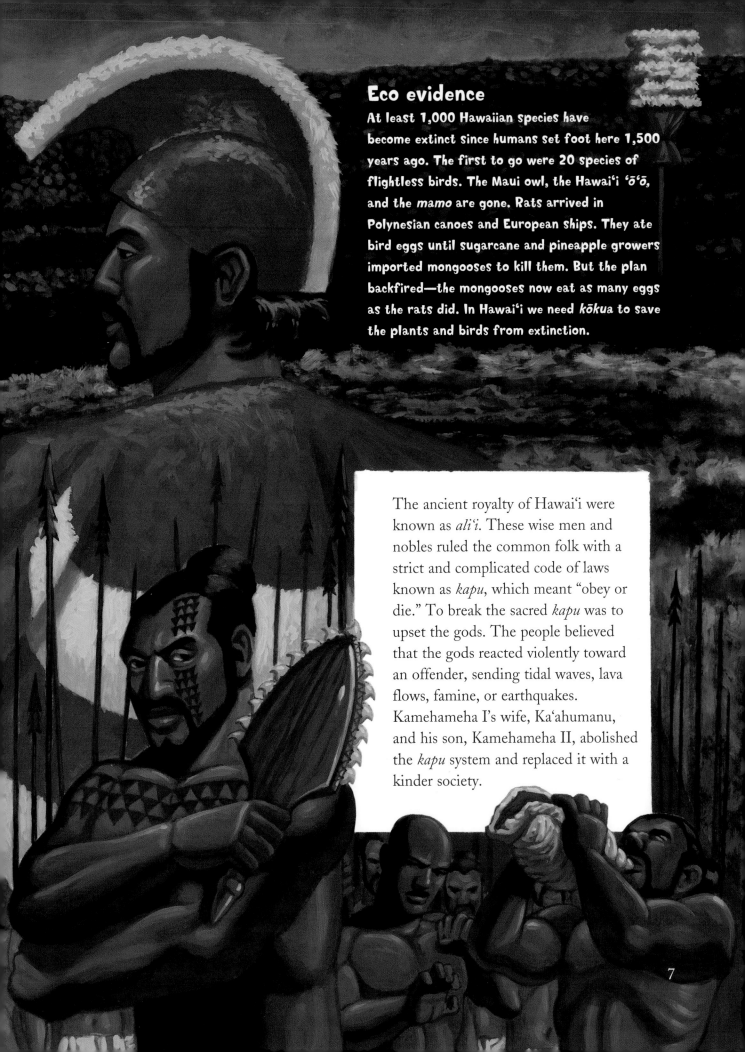

Eco evidence

At least 1,000 Hawaiian species have become extinct since humans set foot here 1,500 years ago. The first to go were 20 species of flightless birds. The Maui owl, the Hawai'i 'ō'ō, and the *mamo* are gone. Rats arrived in Polynesian canoes and European ships. They ate bird eggs until sugarcane and pineapple growers imported mongooses to kill them. But the plan backfired—the mongooses now eat as many eggs as the rats did. In Hawai'i we need *kōkua* to save the plants and birds from extinction.

The ancient royalty of Hawai'i were known as *ali'i*. These wise men and nobles ruled the common folk with a strict and complicated code of laws known as *kapu*, which meant "obey or die." To break the sacred *kapu* was to upset the gods. The people believed that the gods reacted violently toward an offender, sending tidal waves, lava flows, famine, or earthquakes. Kamehameha I's wife, Ka'ahumanu, and his son, Kamehameha II, abolished the *kapu* system and replaced it with a kinder society.

7

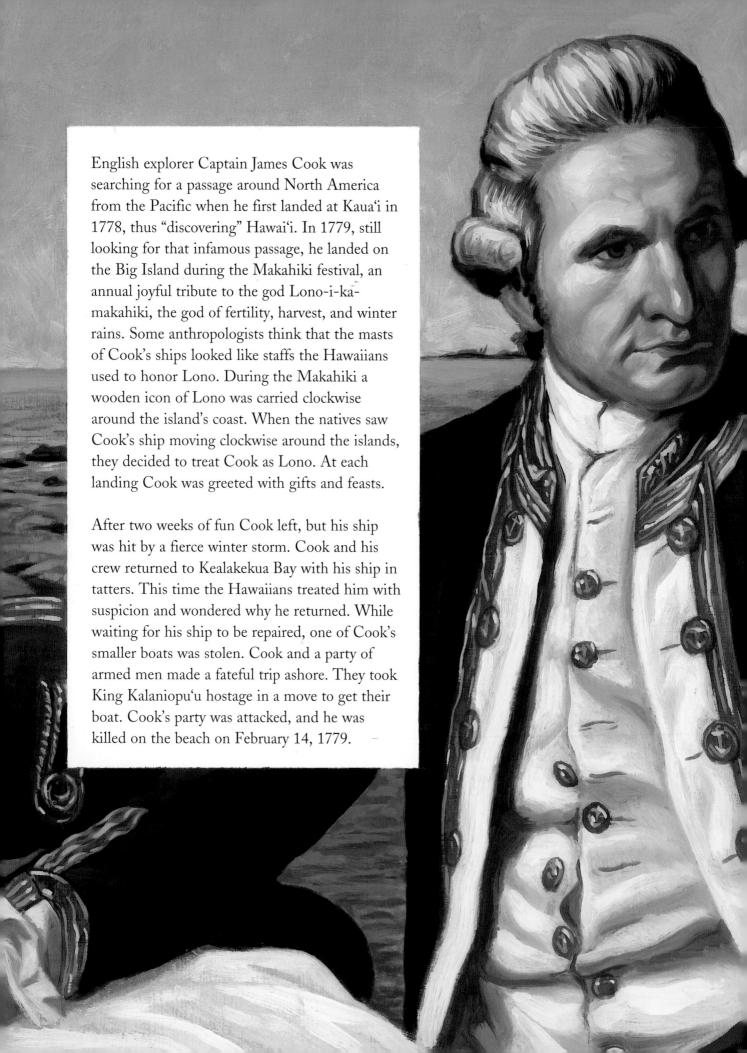

English explorer Captain James Cook was searching for a passage around North America from the Pacific when he first landed at Kaua'i in 1778, thus "discovering" Hawai'i. In 1779, still looking for that infamous passage, he landed on the Big Island during the Makahiki festival, an annual joyful tribute to the god Lono-i-ka-makahiki, the god of fertility, harvest, and winter rains. Some anthropologists think that the masts of Cook's ships looked like staffs the Hawaiians used to honor Lono. During the Makahiki a wooden icon of Lono was carried clockwise around the island's coast. When the natives saw Cook's ship moving clockwise around the islands, they decided to treat Cook as Lono. At each landing Cook was greeted with gifts and feasts.

After two weeks of fun Cook left, but his ship was hit by a fierce winter storm. Cook and his crew returned to Kealakekua Bay with his ship in tatters. This time the Hawaiians treated him with suspicion and wondered why he returned. While waiting for his ship to be repaired, one of Cook's smaller boats was stolen. Cook and a party of armed men made a fateful trip ashore. They took King Kalaniopu'u hostage in a move to get their boat. Cook's party was attacked, and he was killed on the beach on February 14, 1779.

Mea kūʻiʻo

Hawaiʻi used to be called the Sandwich Islands, after the Earl of Sandwich. (Was that a lot of bologna or what?) Captain Cook was the first Westerner to "discover" Hawaiʻi, and since the Sandwich dude paid for part of his trip, Cook named the place after him.

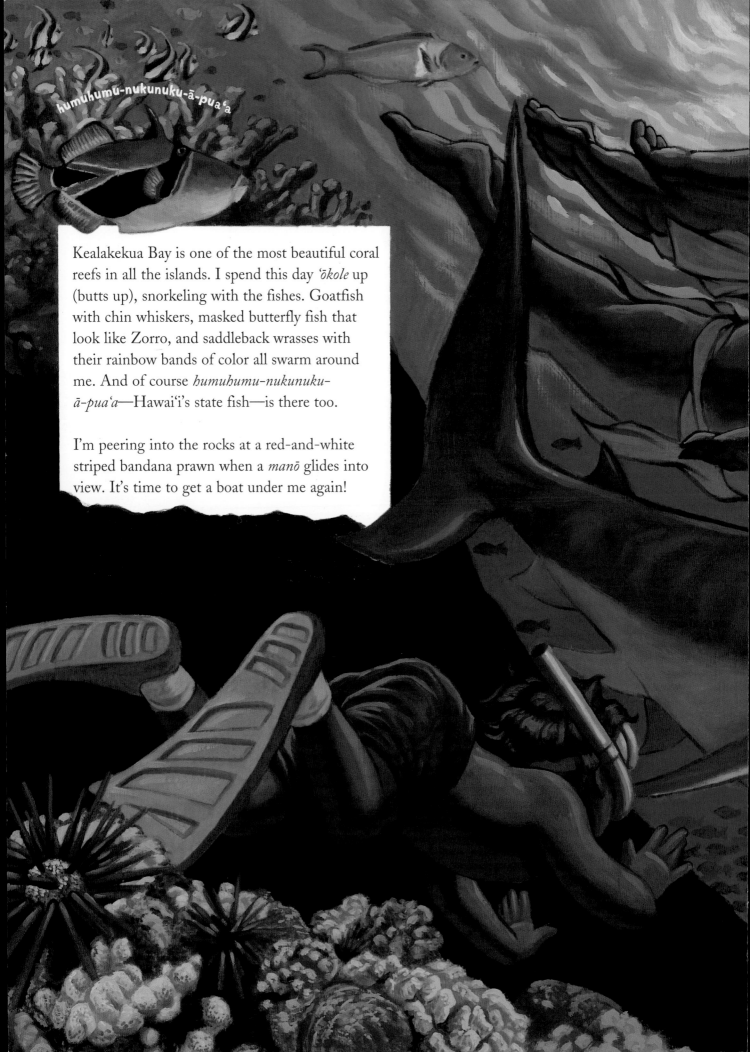

humuhumu-nukunuku-ā-pua'a

Kealakekua Bay is one of the most beautiful coral reefs in all the islands. I spend this day *'ōkole* up (butts up), snorkeling with the fishes. Goatfish with chin whiskers, masked butterfly fish that look like Zorro, and saddleback wrasses with their rainbow bands of color all swarm around me. And of course *humuhumu-nukunuku-ā-pua'a*—Hawai'i's state fish—is there too.

I'm peering into the rocks at a red-and-white striped bandana prawn when a *manō* glides into view. It's time to get a boat under me again!

Eco evidence

Some of these pretty fishes pack a punch. The most amazing is the lionfish, a spiky crimson beauty that has a venomous sting. Don't touch!

Mea kū'i'o

'Aumākua are ancestral gods and can take various animal forms in their roles as protectors and guides. For some Native Hawaiians sharks were 'aumākua and so for them it was kapu to eat shark meat—although that didn't mean you couldn't hunt sharks. When a shark was killed, its bones, skin, and teeth were used to make weapons, sandpaper, and fishhooks.

You know you're in Hawai'i if . . .
you bring your Christmas tree to the beach.

Heading up the eastern coast, we come to
Kapoho, a village wiped clean by the 1960
eruption of Kīlauea. We ditch the kayaks for now
and transform from seafaring wanderers to—
cowboys! The largest private ranch in the USA,
Parker Ranch, is on the Big Island. There's a
rodeo going on. Dad and I eat *poke* and watch
the *paniolo* strut their stuff. Portuguese cowboys
brought the *'ukulele*—a small four- or eight-
stringed guitar with a unique sound—
to the islands.

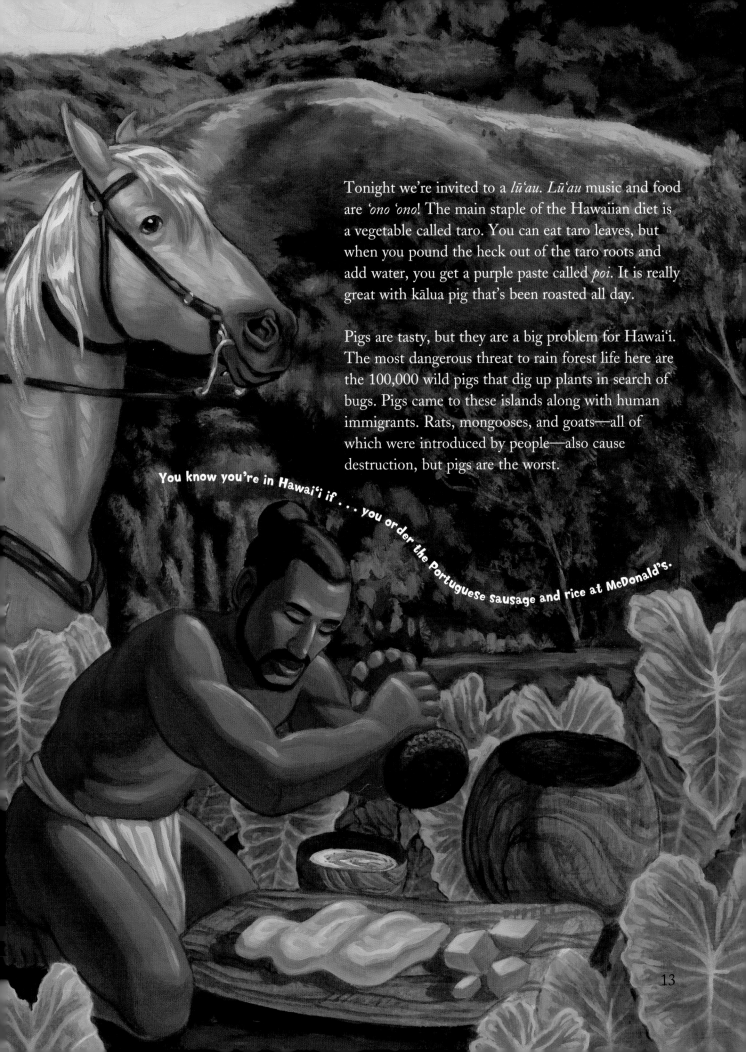

Tonight we're invited to a *lūʻau*. *Lūʻau* music and food are *ʻono ʻono*! The main staple of the Hawaiian diet is a vegetable called taro. You can eat taro leaves, but when you pound the heck out of the taro roots and add water, you get a purple paste called *poi*. It is really great with kālua pig that's been roasted all day.

Pigs are tasty, but they are a big problem for Hawaiʻi. The most dangerous threat to rain forest life here are the 100,000 wild pigs that dig up plants in search of bugs. Pigs came to these islands along with human immigrants. Rats, mongooses, and goats—all of which were introduced by people—also cause destruction, but pigs are the worst.

You know you're in Hawaiʻi if . . . you order the Portuguese sausage and rice at McDonald's.

Kahoʻolawe

The island of Kahoʻolawe was until recently under the control of the U.S. Navy. For 50 years it was used as a practice bombing target. Archaeological evidence shows Kahoʻolawe was inhabited for over a thousand years. People fished, farmed, and lived in the coastal and interior settlements. In ancient times the island was called Kanaloa for the god of the ocean and the foundations of the earth. It is a place where *kāhuna* and navigators were trained for vast Pacific migrations.

Today Kahoʻolawe is a centerpiece for the Native Hawaiian struggle to heal the land and retain their culture. When the island was taken by the government during World War II, the Secretary of the Navy promised it would be restored to a "habitable condition" when it no longer served the Navy's purposes.

The people of Hawaiʻi have fought to see that promise kept. Kahoʻolawe is riddled with unexploded and unstable bombs and ammunitions on shore and off. Once this dangerous junk is gone, erosion must be controlled and native plants reintroduced. The mission of the people is to restore the *kino* to Kahoʻolawe— the spirit of well-being—that recognizes the Hawaiian belief that the land and ocean are living, spiritual entities, refuges and *wahi pana*—sacred places.

Maui

Today we flew into Maui, kayaks and all.

Off the coast of the old whaling town of Lāhainā we spot several humpback whales breaching and tail slapping—having a whale of a time. They're headed for Alaska and a summer of eating herring and krill.

As dusk falls we wander through town, past the Baldwin House—the former home of the first doctor and dentist in Hawai'i—down to the banyan tree. Fifty feet tall, the tree was brought from India in 1873 as an eight-foot sapling. Now it covers a whole block and spreads over an acre!

Next morning we board the narrow-gauge sugarcane train to chug the slopes of the West Maui Mountains. Then we rent some wheels and drive to the Haleakalā Crater, the largest dormant volcano on earth. There we meet up with a mule guide to head down into the desolate landscape inside the crater. It's a misty, bottomless pit filled with lava tubes and bubble caves. The wind whistles over the cinder cones along Sliding Sands Trail. Balloon-shaped silver swords sway back and forth as a *nēnē*, the state bird that flies like a duck and moos like a cow, watches us.

Then we're off to Hāna. Not many tourists here. Unlike the rest of Maui, which is dotted with fancy resorts, Hāna is laid-back. It is known as "the town time forgot" and is the self-proclaimed windsurfing capital of the world.

Eco evidence-

Male humpbacks sing to find a mate. You often hear their voices when diving.

17

Lāna'i

Lāna'i is called the Pineapple Island. It was formed by a single shield volcano and still retains a rounded shape. The island is in a rain shadow, so it doesn't get much rain.

We camp at Shipwreck Beach, and I see one of the weirder transplants to these islands. The spiny-backed spider looks like a morphed hermit crab with red spikes on its back. Its sting hurts but won't kill you (unless you're allergic to it). Another oddball is the carnivorous caterpillar that pretends to be a twig in order to catch fruit flies and other insects. Yuck. And last but not least, I see a Hawaiian happy-face spider. Yup. They have a little smiley face on their back.

Shipwreck Beach is home to a treacherous reef, and lots of sunken ships are here. In the 19th century it was also the dump for old ships. Today it's a gold mine for maritime research. Ancient Hawaiians lived in this area between the 15th and early 19th centuries. Dad and I find petroglyphs on some large lava rocks nearby.

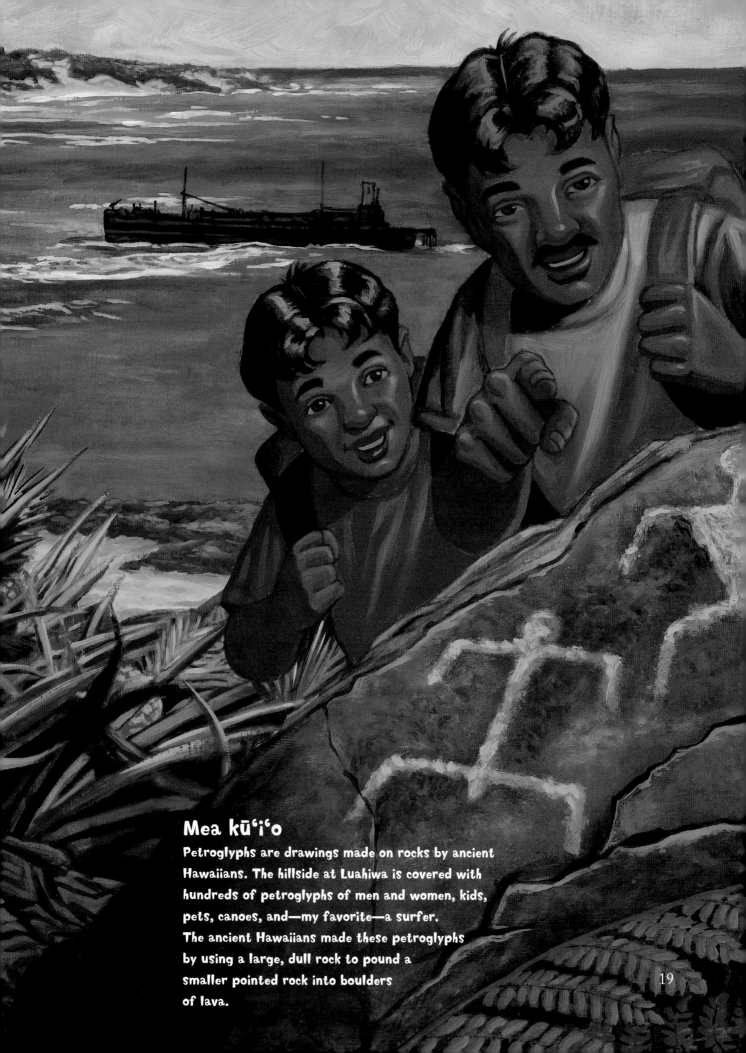

Mea kū'i'o

Petroglyphs are drawings made on rocks by ancient Hawaiians. The hillside at Luahiwa is covered with hundreds of petroglyphs of men and women, kids, pets, canoes, and—my favorite—a surfer. The ancient Hawaiians made these petroglyphs by using a large, dull rock to pound a smaller pointed rock into boulders of lava.

19

Moloka'i

Our next stop is Moloka'i—the Friendly Island—and the Kalaupapa Peninsula. In 1865 the government exiled people with Hansen's disease—commonly known as leprosy—to an isolated area of the island, bordered by high cliffs. Abandoned, with little food or water and less hope, the victims of the then untreatable disease became a mob. They lived in caves and stick huts. Then a missionary named Father Damien showed up. He built homes and a church, and he convinced the government to help the people here. The settlement remains today.

There is a monk seal colony on the shore of Moloka'i. The monk seals and the brown bat are Hawai'i's only mammals that didn't arrive with humans. Monk seals are ultrasensitive; they don't like humans around. We're careful to keep our distance. Even though they are totally protected, monk seals remain one of the most endangered of all seals.

Mea kū'i'o

Legend says that Laka, goddess of the *hula*, gave birth to the dance on Moloka'i at a sacred place in Ka'ana. Now Moloka'i is known as *Moloka'i Ka Hula Piko*—the center of the dance.

You know you're in Hawai'i if . . . it's 70 degrees Fahrenheit and you think it's freezing.

Oʻahu

Our first sight of the island of Oʻahu is the famous cliff at Diamond Head, located east of Honolulu at Waikīkī. The Hawaiian name for Diamond Head is Lēʻahi—it means "brow of *ʻahi.*" Legend says it was named by Pele's little sister, who thought it looked like a yellowfin tuna, or *ʻahi.* Sailors dubbed it Diamond Head because they saw the sparkle of calcite crystals and thought they had found a mountain of diamonds. The Diamond Head Lighthouse is on a steep cliff and is one of the most famous beacons in the Pacific. Once we stash our kayaks, we'll be riding the bus in Honolulu— no mules here.

Almost three-quarters of the people who live in Hawaiʻi live on Oʻahu, a place full of history. It's easy to imagine red-plumed warriors driven over the steep cliffs as they fought for control of the islands; their bodies plummeting on the rocks below, or Japanese Zeros strafing and bombing during World War II.

Honolulu is the heart of Hawaiʻi. The city is called the gathering place and is home to the state government, the university, aquariums, museums, parks, and zoos. At the Bishop Museum we see the 50-foot-long skeleton of a sperm whale and amazing artifacts of daily life: dance costumes with riotous feather headdresses, koa wood clubs used to beat the heads of *kapu* breakers, musical instruments, and farming tools.

The morning of December 7, 1941, was beautiful and cloudless at Pearl Harbor. The USS *Arizona* and 18 other warships of the Pacific Fleet were in the harbor when the Japanese attacked at one minute to 8:00. When the smoke cleared, 3,581 Americans were dead, six ships were sunk in the harbor ooze, and 347 warplanes were scrap metal. The "East wind" (as the Japanese were called) had blown. The Arizona Memorial is a shrine to the Americans who lost their lives. It is a 184-foot alabaster memorial that straddles the sunken ship.

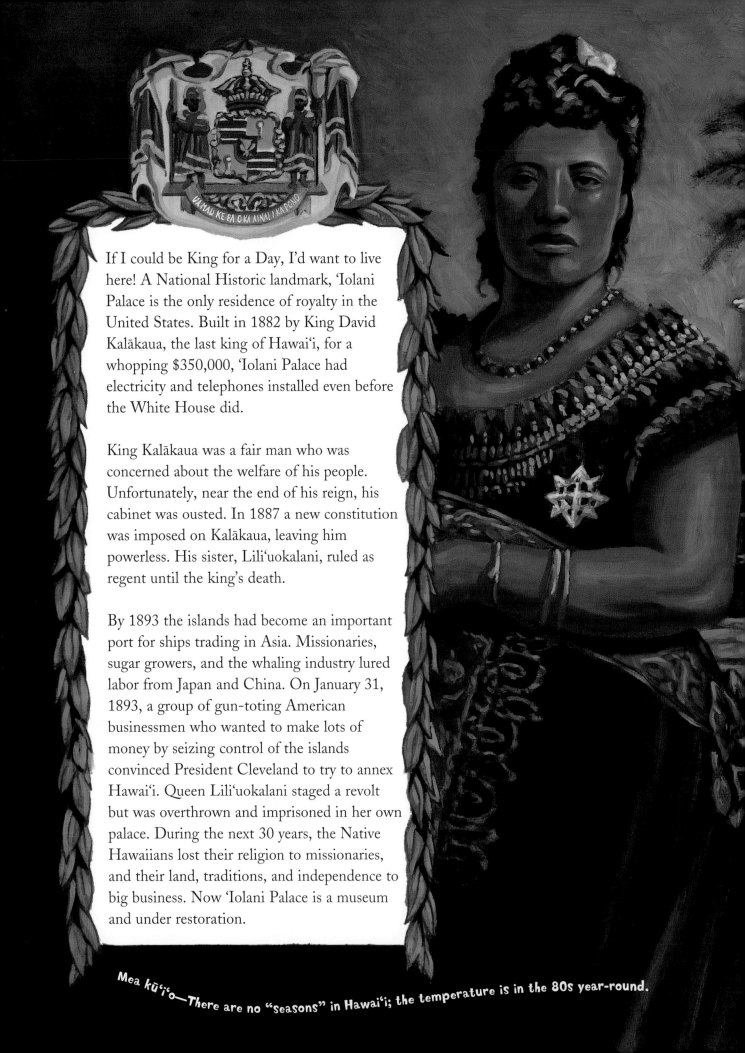

If I could be King for a Day, I'd want to live here! A National Historic landmark, 'Iolani Palace is the only residence of royalty in the United States. Built in 1882 by King David Kalākaua, the last king of Hawai'i, for a whopping $350,000, 'Iolani Palace had electricity and telephones installed even before the White House did.

King Kalākaua was a fair man who was concerned about the welfare of his people. Unfortunately, near the end of his reign, his cabinet was ousted. In 1887 a new constitution was imposed on Kalākaua, leaving him powerless. His sister, Lili'uokalani, ruled as regent until the king's death.

By 1893 the islands had become an important port for ships trading in Asia. Missionaries, sugar growers, and the whaling industry lured labor from Japan and China. On January 31, 1893, a group of gun-toting American businessmen who wanted to make lots of money by seizing control of the islands convinced President Cleveland to try to annex Hawai'i. Queen Lili'uokalani staged a revolt but was overthrown and imprisoned in her own palace. During the next 30 years, the Native Hawaiians lost their religion to missionaries, and their land, traditions, and independence to big business. Now 'Iolani Palace is a museum and under restoration.

Mea kū'i'o—There are no "seasons" in Hawai'i; the temperature is in the 80s year-round.

On the windward side of O'ahu, the air is balmy and perfumed by flowers. This is windsurfer heaven. At Ke'alohi Point we look down over He'eia Fishpond. *He'eia* means "the sliding." It was to Hawaiians the jumping-off point into the spirit world. They believed the souls of the dead came here to leap into eternity. The right side, or He'eia-kea, was the side of light, while the left side, or He'eiāuli, was the domain of darkness. The *kāhuna* said you could actually see the face of God in the sun as it rose over the point.

25

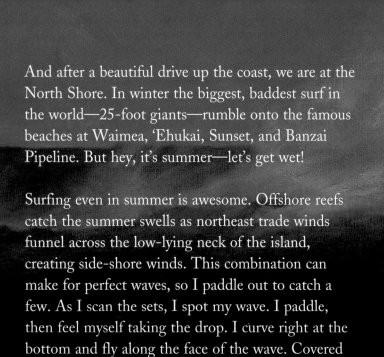

And after a beautiful drive up the coast, we are at the North Shore. In winter the biggest, baddest surf in the world—25-foot giants—rumble onto the famous beaches at Waimea, 'Ehukai, Sunset, and Banzai Pipeline. But hey, it's summer—let's get wet!

Surfing even in summer is awesome. Offshore reefs catch the summer swells as northeast trade winds funnel across the low-lying neck of the island, creating side-shore winds. This combination can make for perfect waves, so I paddle out to catch a few. As I scan the sets, I spot my wave. I paddle, then feel myself taking the drop. I curve right at the bottom and fly along the face of the wave. Covered in salt, warmed by the sun, drenched by the sea . . . hey, I've never had a bad day surfing.

You know you're in Hawai'i if . . . the surf report is on your speed dial.

Mea kūʻiʻo
"Goofy-foot" surfers (right
foot forward) prefer left-breaking waves.

Kaua'i

The Garden Island of Kaua'i is too far to paddle, so we take a quick flight to the oldest of all the islands. Compared to the rugged Big Island, Kaua'i's beauty is soft. The mountains are round and smooth; the jungle dense and tropical. Over time streams have cut deep channels to the sea. In the interior is Waimea Canyon, known as the Grand Canyon of the Pacific. Waterfalls cascade from cliff faces that rise 4,000 feet above the pounding surf. Kaua'i is where Hollywood directors film when the script calls for "paradise." After O'ahu, Kaua'i seems quiet and peaceful.

We hike the Kalalau Trail. The narrow footpath cruises down the Nā Pali Coast through lush valleys and high sea cliffs. It wanders through ancient villages, lava tubes, and caves. We camp and listen to the wind and wonder if Pele will visit her handsome warrior, Lohi'au, while we sleep.

Smack in the middle of the island are Mt. Kawaikini and Mt. Wai'ale'ale. Wai'ale'ale is one of the soggiest spots on earth, with almost 400 inches of rain a year, but just 20 miles away in Waimea it rains only 20 inches a year.

Eco evidence

The bad news is there are cockroaches here the size of your big toe! The good news is the geckos eat them. Geckos chirp at night and are considered good luck—probably 'cuz they eat the cockroaches.

Ni‘ihau

ROBINSON

The saying *Nana I Ke Kumu* means a person must study nature in all its wisdom—in the forests and the streams, the ocean and the air. The early Polynesians took this saying to heart and were sailing around the Pacific in hand-carved canoes with coconut-fiber sails when Europeans were still thinking the world was flat. Polynesians navigated by the stars and assessed the depth of the ocean and currents by the color of the water.

Our last stop is Ni‘ihau, located 17 miles off the southwestern coast of Kaua‘i. Whew! Talk about a rough crossing. But this is the place I really want to see. It's called the Forbidden Island—so naturally I want to be here. We beach at Ki‘i Landing, where residents receive their supplies.

You need special permission to visit Ni‘ihau. Purchased from King Kamehameha the Fifth in 1864 by the Robinson family, this island has preserved many of the traditional ways of life. Today it's inhabited by about 200 Native Hawaiians whose primary language is Hawaiian.

The Niihauans hunt with ropes and knives and fish with spears and nets. Other supplies are brought in by air and sea. There are only a few vehicles on this island; instead, folks ride horses and bicycles. The ocean teems with tropical fish and monk seals, and the water is so clear it's hard to believe your eyes.

I've seen a lot of *da kine,* but I am sleepy as
we return to Kaua'i. We reach Hanalei,
the *lei*-making place. It's just a little village—
you'd miss it if you weren't quick—but it has
the most beautiful bay in the islands. I nap in
a garden filled with plumeria, the favored
flower for making *lei.* A pair of frigate birds
circles above the breaking waves as the soft
touch of the trade winds cools me.

Hawai'i's lush and rugged beauty is what
brings millions of tourists to visit each year.
They spend a bunch of money, but it would
be a shame if we paved paradise in the name
of progress. Finding harmony is the key to
Hawai'i's future. Dad and I had a blast, but
it's time to head back to the Big Island and
our home in Hilo. This is Hawai'i—land of
aloha. Mahalo.